TABLE OF CONTE

Introduction

Chapter 1 **Spices & Herbs: Basics and Background**

Chapter 2 **Spices and Associated Cuisines**

Chapter 3 **Herbs and Associated Cuisines**

Chapter 4 **Cooking with Spices & Herbs**

Chapter 5 **Complementary Combinations**

Chapter 6 **Spice Substitutions**

Chapter 7 **Popular Spice Blend Recipes**

About The Author

INTRODUCTION

Spices and herbs have been used throughout history to bring enhanced flavors, enticing aromas, and attractive colors to foods all over the world. Nevertheless, many home cooks miss easy opportunities to effectively use these ingredients in their cooking routines. A simple lack in knowledge is all that stands in the way of taking your cooking to the next level. By learning some basic principles, you can improve the quality of an average dish or discover endless new culinary possibilities. The distinctive flare of your favorite cuisines can be brought to life by spices and herbs that you may already have in your kitchen.

You will learn what individual spices and herbs can do to enhance your dish and how they can blend and balance with others to create amazing results. Whether you want to find some great substitutions to spices you may not have in your kitchen, flavor pairings with whole foods that cut the guesswork, or great spice blend recipes, this book has you covered. Keep reading to unlock the benefits of nature's most flavorful ingredients. You will be well on your way to preparing more tasty, dynamic, and memorable dishes in no time.

CHAPTER 1
SPICES & HERBS: BASICS AND BACKGROUND

Spices and herbs are derived from plant components and are often considered one in the same. These nature-given ingredients have some important distinguishing features, though. Spices come from the oil-rich seeds, roots, bark, and flowering buds of a plant. The plants which produce most of the spices we enjoy are grown in tropical or subtropical climate zones. Most often, spices are consumed in dried form.

Herbs, on the other hand, are derived from plant leaves. Plants grown in temperate climates are typically the source of many herbs we consume. Unlike spices, herbs are frequently consumed fresh as well as dried. A few plants produce both culinary herbs *and* spices.

A BRIEF HISTORY

Earliest records of spices and herbs reveal a practical focus on medicine, holy oils, and aromatics. Egyptian scrolls from about 1550 B.C. document many of these spices and herbs, including those not native to Egypt. It is apparent that some form of spice trade existed even at this point in history. The precise timing of our first experimentations with spices and herbs in food sources is largely unknown, but there is certainly significant evidence of this practice.

When Egypt was conquered by Alexander the Great, Alexandria became an essential port for spice trade. This opened more opportunity for spice consumption in foods. Spices eventually became so desirable that even valuable resources like silver and gold were traded to acquire them. The Red Sea served as a direct trade route between Rome and India during the first century, which also helped to bring spices to much of Europe. Prior to this, Arab regions had nearly exclusive control of the spice trade.

Gardens of European monasteries were full of both culinary and medicinal herbs around this time. These fine resources also gained popularity as preservatives to assist in longer term food storage. Greeks and Romans were beginning to use poppy seeds to liven up ordinary bread, and spices such as fennel to bring more depth of flavor to their staple vinegar-based sauces. Garlic quickly became a favorite addition to the cooking routines of many due to its amazing versatility and taste.

Romans had an especially enthusiastic reliance on spices and herbs. Many wines in ancient Rome were flavored with full-bodied spices. In the Mediterranean region, spices such as pepper, cinnamon, and ginger were also increasingly consumed.

In 410 A.D., Rome was overtaken by a River tribe who demanded 3,000 pounds of pepper in addition to other valuables to spare Roman lives. The fall of Rome greatly impacted European spice trade, but it was destined to re-surge.

Charlemagne, King of (present-day) France from 742-814, made sure farmers were planting and growing a variety of culinary herbs such as anise, fennel, sage, and thyme. He was the first person of high influence to strongly advocate spice and herb cultivation. Marco Polo detailed spices in his highly influential travel memoirs. His writings are thought to have sparked the acceleration of the international spice trade; around 1300.

During his 1493 voyage, Christopher Columbus was accompanied by Diego Chanca, a Spanish physician. Chanca helped to discover red pepper and allspice, two spices that would become essential in kitchens for years to come. Spices and herbs played a significant role in the formulation of tea substitutions in the American Colonies when drinking traditional tea was labeled as unpatriotic. Chamomile flowers, blackberry leaves, and sassafras bark were used to make these replacement drinks, to name a few.

By the early 1800s, many places around the world were growing spices and had developed plantations. When American commerce became less restricted in the late 18th century, the U.S. became part of the world spice trade. Americans received spices such as pepper, ginger, and cinnamon in exchange for valuable goods like fish, tobacco, and soap.

Today, spices and herbs are used all over the world to enhance the food we eat. Fortunately, monopolies no longer rule the spice trade as they once had. America now leads in spice imports and consumption, but very few spices are grown on American soil due to its unsuitable climate. Many herbs, however, are grown in the United States, and this agricultural industry has been expanding.

America is just one of many places across the globe showing a steady increase in demand for spices linked to other unique cuisines. This is just one indication of the growing fondness for international menu items, and the essential spices and herbs used to prepare them.

Chapter 2
Spices and Associated Cuisines

This Chapter will provide you with detailed descriptions of a variety of spices used around the globe. The lists of commonly linked cuisines by spice are by no means exhaustive.

AJWAIN

Ajwain seeds come from an annual herb native to Asia minor but now grown throughout the Middle East. They have an intense aroma which is sometimes compared with thyme and cumin. These seeds are delicious in starchy foods and blend particularly well with garlic and lemon.

Cuisines: African, Indian

ALLSPICE

Allspice is a dried berry from a tree native to Central America and the West Indies. This spice contains hints of nutmeg, pepper, cloves, and cinnamon-- leading to its fitting name. Understandably, it is often mistaken as a spice blend. Allspice is a prominent component of Jamaican Jerk seasoning.

Cuisines: Cajun & Creole, Caribbean, Latin American, Mexican, Middle Eastern

ANISE

Anise seeds come from a flowering plant within the parsley family. The seeds can be used whole or ground. They have an aroma of licorice and a somewhat fruity flavor. Anise seeds are used to flavor meat dishes and several beverages. They are often consumed with a candy-coating in India and the Netherlands.

Cuisines: German, Italian, Indian, Latin American, Middle Eastern, Mexican

ANNATTO SEED:

This type of seed comes from the achiote tree, native to the Caribbean region. Annatto seeds are usually ground into a paste and infused with oil. The whole seed form is rarely used in recipes. It is often used as a food dye, bringing the yellow color to staples like butter and cheese. When added to foods, the resulting flavor can be described as earthy and somewhat peppery.

Cuisines: Caribbean, Latin American, Mexican

CARAWAY

Caraway seeds are actually the dried fruit of the Carcum carvi, a member of the parsley family. It is often compared to anise and dill, but with a hint of citrus. It is commonly used to flavor sauerkraut, pork, and rye bread, among others.

Cuisines: Cajun & Creole, German, Middle Eastern, Mediterranean

CARDAMOM

Cardamom spice is derived from a dried fruit from plants native to India, in the ginger family. The spice can be used whole or ground. The two main types of cardamom are Mysore and Malabar. Aroma can be described as slightly fruity and bittersweet, while flavor has hints of lemon and mint. It is used in many foods--from baked goods and meat dishes to coffees.

Cuisines: Cajun & Creole, North African, Thai, Mediterranean, Indian, Middle Eastern

CELERY SEED

Celery seed, as expected, comes from the celery plant. They can be consumed ground in addition to seed form. They have a strong and distinct aroma and flavor. Stews, soups, sausages, and pickled foods frequently contain celery seed.

Cuisines: Cajun & Creole, French, German, Russian

CHIA SEEDS

Chia seeds are highly adaptable. They are popular as a superfood because of their high omega 3 content. Their nutty flavor becomes sweeter when in liquid. Chia seeds are frequently used in chocolate, jams, breads, but can also be added to cereals, salads and much more. They are used in an array of cuisines.

CHILI PEPPERS

Chili peppers are fruits originally cultivated in Mexico. A distinctive chemical, capsaicin, protects the seeds and provides their familiar heat factor. This heat level can vary widely from one type of chili pepper to another. In fact, the no-heat favorite bell pepper is part of the chili family. These peppers can be used fresh or dried, often in flake or powdered forms. There are many varieties of chili peppers such as chipotle, poblano, serrano, ancho, and aleppo. (common in Middle Eastern dishes).

Cuisines: Cajun & Creole, Caribbean, Chinese, Latin American, Mediterranean, Mexican, Indian, Middle Eastern, North African, Spanish, Thai

CINNAMON

Cinnamon, the oldest known spice, is derived from the inner bark of the Cinnamomum tree. This tropical tree produces many aromatic compounds, giving this spice its familiar scent and spicy flare. Cinnamon is usually purchased as rolled quills (sticks) or in powdered form. Varieties of cinnamon sold for culinary use include cinnamomum cassia (common in East Asia and the U.S.) and cinnamomum verum. Cinnamon can be a star in both sweet and savory dishes.

Cuisines: Caribbean, Indian, Japanese, Mediterranean, Mexican, Middle Eastern

CLOVES

Cloves are the flower buds of the Syzygium aromaticum tree of Indonesia. This spice has been used in China and Europe for centuries and is well known for its intense aroma. Cloves have a high essential oil content and are filled with more aromatic compounds than any other known spice. Cloves can be used whole or ground. They are often included in savory dishes such as meat roasts but work well in sweeter dishes. Cloves are also used to flavor mulled wines and ciders.

Cuisines: Cajun & Creole, Caribbean, Indian, Japanese, Mediterranean, Middle Eastern, Thai, Spanish

COCOA POWDER

Cocoa powder comes from beans of the cacao tree. This evergreen tree is native to tropical regions of Mexico. Cocoa powder is acidic with a slight bitterness and is typically combined with sugar. It is used in many baked goods and is a secret ingredient in some savory recipes such as steak rubs. Cocoa powder is used within an array of cuisines.

CORIANDER

Coriander seeds are found in the fruit of the same plant that produces the cilantro herb. Coriander can be used when green and fresh or when dried. The dried, commonly used form of coriander can be described as floral with some citrus flavor. It blends well with cumin and can be used in many savory dishes.

Cuisines: Mexican, Mediterranean, Indian, Middle Eastern

CUMIN

Cumin seeds come from dried fruits grown in South Asia. It is often purchased in powder form. It has long been enjoyed around the globe in a variety of cuisines. Cumin has been described as nutty, spicy, and earthy with subtle hints of citrus. It is often used in rice, bean, and vegetable dishes.

Cuisines: Cajun & Creole, Latin American, Mediterranean, Mexican, North African, Thai, Indian, Middle Eastern

DILL SEED

Dill seeds come from the same plant that produces the herb (dill weed) and is native to southeastern Europe and the Mediterranean. Dill is usually associated with dill pickles in the United States but is also popular in cabbage, onion, and potato dishes in Germany and Russia.

Cuisines: Cajun & Creole, German, Russian

FENNEL

Fennel seeds are the tiny dried fruits of the fennel plant. It is found in the Mediterranean and southwest Asia as well as certain parts of the United States. The flavor is frequently compared to that of anise and can also be described as bitter and floral. The fragrance is compared to licorice. It is often used in Italian sausage and can be complementary to other meat dishes.

Cuisines: Chinese, Indian, Mediterranean

FENUGREEK

Fenugreek seeds are derived from a plant in the pea family grown in the Mediterranean. They have a bittersweet and slightly nutty flavor. These seeds can be toasted to help decrease bitterness. Fenugreek is often used in curry powder and in chutneys.

Cuisines: Indian, Mediterranean, Middle Eastern

GARLIC

Garlic is related to the onion and grows in bulb form underground. The plant originated in central Asia. It is one of the mostly popular spices worldwide and can be used fresh or dried. It is easily found in minced, powdered, or in whole form. Garlic is used to add flavor and aroma to a vast array of savory dishes.

Cuisines: Cajun & Creole, Latin American, Mediterranean, Mexican, Caribbean, French, Indian, Thai, Middle Eastern, North African, Russian, Spanish

GINGER

Ginger is derived from the underground stem of a tropical flowering plant called Zingiber officinale. This plant is related to those that produce cardamom and turmeric. When dried and heated, the aromatic compound gingerol becomes sweeter and more palatable. Ground ginger is often used in sweet dishes. Ginger can also be used fresh and is a component of many beverages—including healthy beverages such as probiotic drinks.

Cuisines: Caribbean, Chinese, Japanese, North African, Thai,
Mediterranean, Indian, Middle Eastern

GRAINS OF PARADISE

Grains of paradise are the glossy seeds of the Aframomum melegueta plant.
The plant is part of the ginger family and originated in western Africa. These
seeds have a flavor that can be described as woody and slightly spicy which
allows them to be an ideal substitute for black pepper. This spice is also used
for pickling and for brewing certain varieties of beer.

Cuisines: North African

HORSERADISH POWDER

Horseradish powder is a spice derived from the horseradish root vegetable. It
is native to western Asia and southeastern Europe. In powdered form, it can
be used to add a warm zing to sauces, as well as meat dishes. It is used in a
variety of cuisines.

JUNIPER BERRIES

Juniper berries are not true berries; they are the small cones of the juniper
bush. This plant grows in northern climate zones. The berries can be crushed
or toasted to release more flavor. They have a flavor profile sometimes
compared to that of rosemary. Both citrus and piney notes can be detected.
Juniper berries can be used in variety of sauces, marinades, lamb dishes and
beverages.

Cuisines: French, German

MACE

Mace is the outer covering of nutmeg; derived from an evergreen tree native
to Indonesia. Mace is typically ground and dried for culinary use. It is often
used along with nutmeg in spice blends but has a slightly sweeter flavor
profile than its nutmeg counterpart. This spice is most often used in baked
goods.

Cuisines: Cajun & Creole, Caribbean, Indian, Mediterranean, Thai

MUSTARAD SEED

Mustard seed is found in three varieties—Mediterranean yellow/white mustard (most popular in the U.S.), Himalayan brown mustard, and black mustard (most pungent). The sulfur compounds responsible for the slight "burning" effect are called thiocyanates. Onions, horseradish, and wasabi contain these compounds as well. If mustard seeds are cooked, these compounds have a decreased effect. Whole mustard seeds are typically used for pickling, while ground mustard is often added to sauces.

Cuisines: Cajun & Creole, Chinese, German, Indian

NIGELLA

Nigella seeds are also known as black cumin. They can be found in Asia, Africa, and the Mediterranean. The aroma has been compared to that of fennel while flavors of oregano and nutmeg are noticeable. These seeds are commonly roasted and added to curries and vegetable-based dishes. They are most popular in India and the Middle East.

Cuisines: Indian, Middle Eastern

NUTMEG

Nutmeg comes from the ripened fruits of an evergreen tree native to Indonesia. This spice contains compounds that are also found in mace. It is most often ground for culinary purposes and used in a variety of baked goods. Nutmeg also makes a great addition to some savory dishes including tomato sauce and lamb.

Cuisines: Cajun & Creole, Caribbean, French, Indian, Mediterranean, Mexican, Middle Eastern, Spanish, Thai

PAPRIKA

Paprika is a type of powdered chili (described previously). It is most often found in ground form and has a mild, or a slightly smoky flavor. Domestic paprika can be described as somewhat sweet.

Cuisines: Cajun & Creole, Latin American, Mediterranean, North African, Cajun, Indian, Spanish

PEPPERCORNS

Peppercorns are fruits that are produced by the Piper nigrum plant. This plant is native to the Indian subcontinent. There are black, green, and white peppercorn varieties based on maturity. Black peppercorns are most intense in flavor. Green peppercorns are immature and milder. White peppercorns are simply black peppercorns with the outer husk removed. The area in which the peppercorn was grown can create subtle differences in flavor. Peppercorns are a spice cabinet staple found in kitchens across the globe.

Cuisines: Cajun & Creole, Caribbean, Chinese, Indian, Japanese, Mediterranean, Middle Eastern, Thai

SAFFRON

Saffron is the pistil or stigma of the autumn crocus flower which is believed to have its origins in Greece. Harvesting this part of the flower is a meticulous process. As a result, saffron is the most expensive spice in the world and is frequently counterfeited. Saffron has a threadlike form and a uniquely subtle and slightly sweet taste with a full aroma.

Cuisines: Cajun & Creole, Indian, Latin American, North African, Mediterranean, Spanish

STAR ANISE

Star Anise is a fruit produced by trees native to China and Vietnam. It has a star shape; usually with eight points. Despite the similarity in name, it is not related to anise seed. It can be used whole or ground. The flavor is relatively sweet. Star anise is responsible for the sweetness in Chinese five-spice powder. In the United States, star anise is used similarly to cloves.

Cuisines: Chinese, Indian, Latin American

SUMAC

Sumac comes from shrub fruits native to the Mediterranean. Typically ground, this spice is tangy and has some hints of pine and citrus. It is popular in the Middle East and in North Africa where it is commonly added to hummus, salads, meats and fish.

Cuisines: Middle Eastern, North African

TURMERIC

Turmeric is derived from the underground stem portion (rhizome) of the Curcuma longa plant. This flowering plant is in the ginger family and has origins in India. Turmeric is ground and has a bright orange-yellow hue. Its flavor can be described as earthy with detectable notes of mustard and pepper. Turmeric is often used in curry powders, Worcestershire sauce, and yellow mustard (largely for coloring).

Cuisines: Chinese, Indian, Japanese, Mediterranean, Middle Eastern, North African, Thai

VANILLA

Vanilla beans grow on an orchid of the genus Vanilla. There are many species of Vanilla; but the most popular types are grown in Mexico, Tahiti, and Madagascar. Besides the flavor compound vanillin, there are 200 other aromatic compounds found in this spice. Vanilla extract is processed after a lengthy curing process where vanilla beans release their aroma. Saffron is the only spice with a higher price tag than vanilla; but despite this, vanilla remains a favorite addition to many desserts and beverages.

CHAPTER 3
HERBS AND ASSOCIATED CUISINES

This Chapter will provide you with descriptions of a variety of herbs used around the globe. The lists of commonly linked cuisines by herb are by no means exhaustive.

BASIL

Basil has origins in India and there are around 50 recognized species of the plant. It is commonly grown in California, Egypt, and France. Examples of basil varieties include sweet, Thai, and lemon basil. Basil flavor has been compared to mint, pepper, and anise. It is used both fresh and dried for culinary purposes and is a popular spice in Italian dishes and pesto. It is also used in some savory desserts and in cocktails.

Cuisines: Cajun & Creole, Italian, Thai, Mediterranean, Mexican, Spanish

BAY LEAVES

Bay leaves are dried leaves of a tree belonging to the laurel family. These leaves are usually purchased whole for culinary use. They are most commonly cooked in stews, soups, and sauces to release flavor and taken out of the dish prior to serving. Flavor can be described as earthy, with hints of clove and nutmeg.

Cuisines: Cajun & Creole, German, Latin American, Mediterranean, Indian, Middle Eastern, Spanish

CHERVIL

Chervil, also known as French parsley, is a delicate springtime herb. It has a light flavor which can be compared to parsley or tarragon. Chervil is often used in egg dishes, salads, and soups, and can make a beautiful garnish.

Cuisines: French, Russian, German

CHIVES

Chives are related to garlic and onions. The green stem portion of the chive functions as an herb. They are often used fresh but can also be chopped and dried. Chives make a great garnish but also contribute flavor to an array of savory dishes with their mild onion taste. Chives are an easy herb to grow on your own if they are provided adequate sunlight and water.

Cuisines: Cajun & Creole, French, German, Italian, Russian, Mediterranean

CILANTRO

Cilantro leaves come from the coriander plant, which is a member of the parsley family. Cilantro does not hold up well to drying and is most often used while fresh. Flavor is described as peppery, citrusy, and sometimes pungent. Cilantro has a reputation for tasting "soapy" to many, due to the naturally occurring aldehyde chemical in the leaves. This spice is widely used in Mexican and Asian dishes and can be found in many recipes for salsas, soups, and dips.

Cuisines: Caribbean, Latin American, Mexican, Thai, North African

DILL WEED

Dill weed is an herb with origins in Europe and Asia. It is used both fresh and dried. Dried dill weed has a significantly milder taste. Dill weed has a unique flavor that is an acquired taste for some. It is often used conservatively in recipes other than salads, dressings, and dips. Dill weed can also make an appealing garnish.

Cuisines: Cajun & Creole, German, Mediterranean, Middle Eastern, Russian

EPAZOTE

Epazote is an herb derived from a plant native to Central America. Both the leaves and stem are used for culinary purposes. Epazote is primarily called for in Mexican cooking, with a flavor that is described as pungent, sometimes even 'medicinal,' with undertones of anise and mint. It is used both fresh and dried, however, the dried form of epazote results in milder flavor. Epazote is added to many traditional Mexican foods.

Cuisines: Mexican

FILE POWDER

File powder comes from dried sassafras leaves. Sassafras trees grow wild in Canada and the Eastern United States. File powder is often used as a thickener, but it can also contribute to the flavor profile of a dish by adding some earthiness and a slightly fruity aroma. File powder is frequently used to thicken and flavor Creole gumbo.

Cuisines: Cajun & Creole

KAFFIR LIME (LEAVES)

Kaffir limes, a lime variety with a bumpy outer layer, are known for their intense bitterness. The leaves of this tree are used as a culinary herb and are typically available fresh, frozen, or in dry form. They can be placed whole into soups and stir-fries to release flavor or finely cut and used in sauces or toppings. Kaffir lime leaves are very fragrant and flavorful, bringing a bright and fresh appeal to their dishes.

Cuisines: Caribbean, Thai, Indian

LAVENDER

Lavender buds can be used as a culinary herb. English lavender is often favored over French lavender for culinary use as it is slightly sweeter, though some palates prefer the potency of French lavender. Lavender can be used dried or fresh. Dried lavender essence is significantly stronger. Regardless, lavender should be used conservatively in recipes as a small amount goes a long way in delivering both flavor and aroma. This herb has been used in baked goods, fruit pairings, ice cream, and even dry rubs for meats.

Cuisines: French, Japanese

LEMONGRASS

Lemongrass herb is derived from the stalk of the Lemongrass plant. The plant is native to Asia. It can be used fresh or dried, though fresh form is generally preferred to allow more brightness and complexity to transfer into the dish. Hints of lemon, ginger, and mint can be detected. Lemongrass is often added to traditional Thai dishes, as well as to herbal teas and some cocktails.

LOVAGE

The leaves of the lovage plant are valued as an herb, though the root and seeds also have culinary purposes. Lovage is thought to have origins in Europe and is related to dill, carrots, and caraway. Leaves look like flat parsley and flavor can be described as a blend of celery and parsley. Lovage is mostly added to meat dishes, soups, stocks, and salads.

Cuisines: Mediterranean

MARJORAM

Marjoram is an aromatic herb native to the Mediterranean and North Africa. It is part of the mint family. It can be used fresh or dried; salad dressings and meat dishes commonly include dried marjoram. Fresh marjoram works well in vegetable dishes. Flavor is slightly woody with floral and citrus hints.

Cuisines: Cajun & Creole, German, Mediterranean, Italian

MEXICAN OREGANO

Mexican oregano is an herb from a plant in the mint family, unlike the well-known Greek oregano. This variety of oregano is slightly stronger in flavor and has notes of licorice and citrus. It is used traditional Mexican dishes such as soups and tacos.

Cuisines: Latin American, Mexican

MINT

Both spearmint and peppermint aromatic herbs have culinary value within a variety of cuisines. Spearmint has more versatility since its flavor profile is more mellow than peppermint. Mint plants are native to the eastern Mediterranean. Mint can be used fresh, dried, or as an essential oil extraction for its flavor and aroma. This herb has been used in baked goods, sauces, hot drinks, and cocktails.

Cuisines: Indian, Mediterranean, Mexican, North African, Spanish, Thai

OREGANO

Oregano plants yield small, highly fragrant leaves and edible pink flowers. The plant has origins in the Mediterranean. In the Mediterranean, oregano is commonly called wild marjoram, though it is different from the actual marjoram herb. Oregano can be added to dishes fresh or dried though it is mostly used in dried form. It is a familiar ingredient in Italian dishes such as pizza and a variety of pastas.

Cuisines: Cajun & Creole, French, Italian, Latin American, Mediterranean, Middle Eastern, Spanish

PARSLEY

Parsley is a plant native to the Mediterranean that includes two culinary varieties—flat and curly leaf. Parsley has a very light, fresh taste and fragrance and is therefore highly versatile. It can be added to nearly any savory dish and is one of the most common ingredients in Middle Eastern cooking. Fresh parsley is often used as an inviting garnish.

Cuisines: Cajun & Creole, German, Italian, Mediterranean, Middle Eastern, Russian, Spanish

ROSEMARY

Rosemary comes from an aromatic evergreen bush within the mint family. It has origins in the Mediterranean. This herb is a great complement to an array of meat dishes including lamb, pork, chicken, and wild game. It also is used in dairy foods like cheeses and butter.

Cuisines: Cajun & Creole, French, Latin American, Mediterranean, Spanish

SAGE

Sage is a shrub native to the Mediterranean. When it comes to culinary use, the variety known as common sage (or garden sage) is favored. Sage has a distinct savory and earthy flavor. It can be bought fresh or dried, in whole leaf form or rubbed. It is well-known for its role in seasoning sausage though it pairs well with many meats. Rice and bean dishes and tomato sauces often include sage.

SHISO

Shiso comes from the mint family and has origins in China and India. It consists of green and reddish-purple varieties. This herb is often used fresh. Flavor can be described as slightly minty, bitter, and with hints of lemon. It can be used as a cooking wrap for fish and vegetables, and it is often found garnishing sushi rolls.

Cuisines: Japanese, Middle Eastern, Mediterranean, Thai

SUMMER SAVORY

Summer savory is an herb originally grown in the eastern Mediterranean. It has a strong flavor that can be compared to oregano, marjoram, and thyme. It can be dried, but most recipes call for fresh summer savory. It is a key ingredient in the French spice mixture, Herbes de Provence. Summer savory is also commonly added to cooked green beans, stews, and meat pies.

Cuisines: Cajun & Creole, French, Mediterranean

TARRAGON

Tarragon is native to Russia and Asia but is frequently used in French cuisine. It is found and consumed fresh or dried. Tarragon has a unique flavor with light hints of anise and mint. It is often used within herb blends and as a key ingredient in sauces and vinaigrettes. The subtlety of tarragon also works well with many fish and chicken dishes.

Cuisines: Cajun & Creole, French, Mediterranean, Russian, Spanish

THYME

Thyme is an herb consisting of small leaf clusters. It has origins in the Mediterranean and there are a few varieties. This herb can be used fresh or dried, but the dried form should be rehydrated during the cooking process to express its flavor fully. Thyme has woody, floral, and citrus notes. It is used in many cuisines--in soups, stews, stuffing, and a variety of savory meat and vegetable dishes.

Cuisines: Cajun & Creole, Caribbean, French, German, Latin American, Mediterranean, Mexican, Spanish

CHAPTER 4
COOKING WITH SPICES & HERBS

Now it is time to dive into some practical applications so that you can get these ingredients to deliver their value. There are endless possibilities and suggested methods when it comes to cooking with spices and herbs. However, some are foundational to building your own skill and style while also getting great results.

If you are new to cooking with spices and herbs, begin with those that are widely used. Cinnamon, black pepper, basil, and oregano are a few good examples that have good versatility. To most effectively cook with these and any other spice or herb, you need to build a familiarity with the flavor profile. One effective way to get familiar with a certain spice or herb is to mix it with a small amount butter or cream cheese and allow the mixture to sit for at least an hour before sampling on something bland, like a plain cracker or piece of toast.

If a spice or herb is completely new to you, this is an important step, since you will want to keep in mind the overall strength and dominance of the spice or herb to determine its impact. You can simply read about its general impact to build an understanding, but nothing will replace experiential knowledge. This practice will also help you determine your individual tastes and preferences. I believe that your level of successful diversity in cooking and baking will be highly dependent on your willingness to be an open-minded taste tester!

To provide some context, though, spices like bay leaf, ginger, pepper, rosemary, and sage are widely considered to be examples of dominant spices. As such, they should be used more conservatively, especially when you are new to cooking with them. Hot, peppery spices should also be used carefully.

Some examples of medium strength spices and herbs include celery seed, garlic, and turmeric. These may be used less conservatively but can still potentially overpower a dish. Delicate flavors include that of chives, parsley, and basil. These can be used in larger quantities, and work very well in combination with many other spices and herbs. Again, the best way to really gain an understanding of strength and effect is to taste test and to compare.

Spice Tips

Remember that spices are almost always dried long before consumption. As a result, many ground spices may already be somewhat stale upon purchase. The natural oils dissipate, and both color and flavor fade.

The most ideal way to maximize freshness of spices is to buy them whole. Whole spices last longer, and they taste better when you freshly grind them just prior to cooking. It may sound like a major inconvenience, but the payoff is worth the effort.

You can use a mortar and pestle to grind whole spices; or simply use a small plastic storage bag and a meat mallet to crush spices if you do not have one. Purchasing an actual spice grinder is probably the best option, but you can also use an inexpensive coffee grinder and get similar results. In order to maximize the life and flavor of your spices, seriously consider grinding your own. You will taste the difference and experience the benefits right away-- with minimal effort.

Toasting your spices is another way to boost flavor and really wake up the fragrant oils. Some chefs even consider this to be a critical step. Whole or ground spices may be toasted, but there are some considerations for each.

Whole spices can be heated in a dry pan over medium heat. Keep the pan moving and stir spices to avoid scorching, which can happen very quickly. Spices that are different sizes should be toasted in separate batches so smaller spices do not scorch before larger ones are finished. You can stop toasting once the spices become fragrant; they will usually undergo some color change as well.

Some whole spices that are particularly well suited for toasting include cloves, mustard seed, star anise, cinnamon, cumin, fennel seeds, juniper berries, and peppercorns. Toasted whole spices are often used when pickling. Smaller whole spices are often toasted and used in delicious spice blends. You can try this when mixing up one of the spice blend recipes in the last chapter. If you toast too many whole spices for your dish, don't worry. They will keep their toasty, amplified flavor for one to two weeks if stored well (more on this below).

After toasting whole spices, you can also go ahead and either crush or grind them if this form is best for your dish or signature spice blend. Crushed textures are ideal for meat rubs and grilling and ground spices will take your dressings, baked goods, and stews to another level. Before grinding spices, though, let them cool to avoid releasing too much of the aromatics too quickly when creating this finer texture.

Pre-ground spices can be toasted as well, but with extra care. First, they should be mixed with a small amount of cooking liquid (preferably a liquid you will be using in your recipe) to create a paste. Heat some oil in a pan and add the paste; stirring until the liquid has evaporated and the spices release their aromas. Again, spices scorch quickly so be careful not to toast for too long.

Toasted or not, spices will generally release more flavor with longer cooking times. Just avoid adding intense heat too quickly and for too long. You need to be mindful and pay attention--there is really no way around that if you want to ensure a high-quality finished product. Also, it is important to note that flavor development accelerates whenever spices are heated within oils and fats.

Don't forget that whole spices especially lend themselves to prolonged cooking times due to their form, so their flavor has time to be fully extracted and distributed. The whole spice can often be removed from the dish prior to serving. This is usually the case when preparing a long-simmering dish with whole bay leaves, for example.

HERB TIPS

As for herbs, it is almost always worth the trip to the market to buy and use them while fresh. They provide more aroma, color, and a flavor that cannot be completely replicated. There is nothing wrong with using dried herbs, however, as these are practical and convenient to use. The key to cooking herbs effectively, whether fresh or dried, is timing. Dried herbs should be added early in the cooking process, and fresh herbs should be added near the end.

You can do some simple prep work to get the most out of your herbs before adding them to the heat. Prepare dried herbs by crumbling and crushing them a bit to boost flavor. This would ideally be done whether you plan to heat the dried herbs or not. When preparing your fresh herbs for cooking, kitchen shears can be a better alternative to a knife. Shears will create a fine chop to increase surface area exposure, with easier handling. Be aware that herbs softer in structure can easily turn into a paste if they are chopped a little too finely. Herbs such as mint, tarragon, dill, cilantro, and basil are some examples. These will hold up best when more coarsely chopped.

Fresh herbs are added later because they contain more volatile oils and do not need as much time to release flavor. Here again, it is best to keep in mind the delicacy of the herb in terms of both structure and taste. Delicate herbs are especially prone to overheating and flavor loss if put into the dish too early. Texture loss will also occur in this case; negatively impacting the visual appeal. Delicate fresh herbs will be discussed in more detail later.

Dried herbs lose some natural oil content through the dehydration process, but the remaining oils can be quite concentrated. They take more time to release—so, dried herbs should be added early. Dried herbs often end up possessing a deeper, more intense, and in some cases a slightly smoky flavor when they are prepared and cooked properly. This intensity can vary between herbs.

It will be helpful to gain a working knowledge of *resinous* and *delicate* herb types to better understand how they hold up to the cooking process, dried or fresh.

Resinous herbs contain more volatile oils by volume. They have a rigid structure and are less likely to bruise. Some examples include sage, rosemary, thyme, oregano, and marjoram. These herbs become especially intense when dried. Fresh forms are also generally stronger in flavor when compared to the delicate herbs.

Delicate herbs (also known as fine herbs) have a lower volatile oil content and do not carry the same intensity when dried. They typically have a tender structure and are more prone to bruising and damage. Such herbs include mint, tarragon, dill, parsley, and basil. These herbs would be most appreciated in fresh form if possible. Overall heating times should be very minimal. Many delicate herbs can also be served raw within a dish, consumed on the side plainly, or used as an eye-catching garnish.

Some delicate herbs undergo quite noticeable flavor change when they are dried--in addition to flavor loss. This doesn't mean the flavor is poor, but there is a distinction from the fresh flavor. Dill, basil, and parsley are good examples. Again, these herbs would ideally be used when fresh.

Sometimes dried herbs are the preference, outside of considering the assumed convenience factor. For instance, oregano is a dried herb that tends to provide a very long-lasting depth of flavor and is frequently preferred dried over its fresh counterpart.

Resinous herbs *(robust): rosemary, thyme, oregano, marjoram, savory, sage, bay leaf*

Delicate herbs*: basil, parsley, chervil, tarragon, mint, chives, dill*

If you are substituting your dried herbs for fresh ones or vice versa, keep in mind this rule of thumb. You need three times the amount or measurement of fresh herb compared to its dried counterpart.

So, if a recipe asks for one tablespoon of a fresh herb, replace this with one teaspoon of the dried herb (three teaspoons equals one tablespoon).

TASTING

We already discussed tasting as it relates to individual spices and herbs, but one mistake often made is neglecting to taste the dish as it is cooking. This is just as important. To remind yourself, each time you are cooking up something in the kitchen, place a small bowl or saucer beside your work area and use it to sporadically sample your food!

This mistake is so easily fixed. Flavor can deepen, flatten, or otherwise transform as you are cooking, so you should keep in touch with how the dish is developing. This is especially true if you have gained enough knowledge to go freestyle and experiment without any guidance from a recipe. By the way, this is great to do and will accelerate your learning. If you are using a recipe, some cooks recommend adding half the seasonings early in the process; and divide the remaining half into portions to then add incrementally; tasting as you go.

Pay attention to any specifications on introduction times if they are given, though. This will be based on how the individual ingredient will release its flavor relative to other components.

A note on salads and other cold foods… the prolonged flavor release of dried herbs is especially important to remember when using dried herbs in cold foods—it can take hours for the targeted taste to translate through. So, in cold foods like dressings and dips, mix in the dried herbs and allow food to sit a few hours, or even overnight.

On Salt & Pepper...

Salt and pepper are sometimes considered boring or basic. But don't be fooled—this in no way means non-essential. The truth is, most dishes cry out for some good ol' salt and pepper—not instead of, but in addition to the other taste boosting spices and herbs available.

As you know, black pepper is classified as a spice. Salt is a mineral, so it does not belong to either category. Since it is so essential to the culinary arts though, it is more than worth mentioning.

In most cases, salt should be added gradually throughout the cooking process, in increments. This will keep the dish from coming across as too superficially salty. This is particularly true with meats. Salt will permeate through raw meat much better than a cut of meat that has been cooked. Sometimes, the objective is to use salt to help draw moisture content out of foods. This common technique allows savory juices to be extracted from onions, garlic, or other aromatic veggies with high water content. The juices later serve to coat and flavor additional parts of the dish. Again, continue to taste.

There are other considerations. Remember that some ingredients are naturally saltier than others and take this into account when you are adding salt. If your dish has multiple ingredients with moderate salt content to begin with, allow cooking to progress, taste, and add salt later to avoid going overboard. Again, add salt in increments. It is much simpler to contribute than to reduce it if too much was used too early.

All of that aside, do not hesitate to salt what you cook and remember that some whole foods and fresh produce have little to no salt content to start. Sure, some individuals need to be mindful of their salt intake, and there are alternatives that allow for some salt reduction while boosting flavor. Lemon juice is great for this, as well as savory spices and herbs such as garlic, cumin, ginger, tarragon, and oregano. There are also many savory spice blends that can be used (more on this later). However, a dish completely void of salt is likely to fall flat. A well-placed dose of salt will greatly enhance your culinary creation and is also vital to a great marinade (more on this in

Chapter 5).

Good quality black pepper can be just as important. The real key is in the form. It's easy to grab some pre-ground pepper at the grocery store, but you would be surprised at the lack of flavor this provides when compared to the zippy goodness of freshly ground black pepper. You don't have to spend a lot on a fancy grinder as discussed earlier. In fact, you can find whole peppercorns packaged and sold in a glass grinder and ready to go. The texture provided by grinding peppercorns is another reason to make the switch. The crunch and aesthetic of this method can be especially appreciated on premium steaks, buttery baked potatoes, and fresh salads, to name a few.

STORAGE TIPS

To get the most out of your spices and herbs, take some time to learn storage basics. They will go far in helping you preserve the taste and aroma you expect. These tips are simple to learn and apply.

DRIED

Both dried spices and herbs should be stored in containers with tight fitting lids, and they should not be kept too close to the oven and stovetop (despite this being a popular location). The excessive heat and moisture that can come from this area is detrimental to their quality. Many home cooks shake their spices and herbs directly into the dish while it is cooking. This also allows steam and significant moisture to enter the container which again can reduce quality.

If stored well, dried and ground spices will last up to two years. However, some ground spices lose potency in as little as four to eight months. Whole spices and seeds last much longer; up to four years if stored properly. An exception to this general rule is poppy and sesame seeds, which only last for about two years. All of this considered, again, it is certainly worth making the switch to whole spices and grinding them as needed.

Dried herbs do best in stainless steel and glass containers. Too much light exposure can cause these herbs to lose any remaining color quickly, in addition to zapping the strength of their natural oils. Dried herbs last for 1 to 2 years when stored well.

FRESH

Fresh herbs require more attention when it comes to storage. First off, wilted leaves should be removed, and stems should be trimmed slightly. Your herbs will last longer if you wrap the stems in a damp paper towel and place them in a plastic bag before putting them in the refrigerator. This method usually works best with herbs that have a more rigid structure. Examples include oregano, marjoram, rosemary, and thyme.

Delicate fresh herbs, such as basil, cilantro, and parsley, may do better if they are wrapped in a dry or only slightly damp paper towel and placed inside a plastic bag with small holes. This will allow some moisture to escape to avoid sogginess. Another option for tender herbs is to place them upright in a jar with about an inch of water. Then, use a resealable bag or plastic wrap to cover the herbs exposed above the jar. Place the jar in the refrigerator. It is worth noting that basil is particularly sensitive to the cold; and should be stored at room temperature.

If you take some time to store fresh herbs properly, herbs like mint, sage, savory, and basil will last about two weeks. You'll get three weeks of life out of parsley, dill, cilantro, tarragon, and rosemary. Chives will remain relatively fresh for about one week.

Be sure to remove any ties or bands on the herbs and separate them into smaller sections for storage. Also, keep the herbs in a spot easily seen in the refrigerator, so they are not forgotten. When you see mold and notice excessive brittleness, it is time to toss the herbs.

Many people avoid buying and using fresh herbs because they do not last long and may end up wasted as a result. Instead of completely missing out on the benefits of fresh herbs in your cooking, try to plan meals for the week, at least now and then. Use the herbs in at least two or three of the meals you have planned.

Chapter 5
Complementary Combinations

The following lists show spices and herbs that can complement and enhance a variety of vegetables and meats. *The spice and herb lists for each vegetable and meat variety is not intended to be a blend (thought they may spark ideas for great blends). Rather, it is a guide to individual flavors that will make satisfying additions to specific vegetables and meats.*

If you are in the mood to do some creative experimentation, these lists will serve as a great tool to help you jump right in and start discovering amazing flavor combinations. Or, just pick one (or a few) of the spices under a given vegetable or meat, type it into the search field within your browser, and I'm sure you will find some great online recipes to try out. You may discover other great spices and herbs to add to your vegetables and meats depending on your individual taste.

Don't miss the marinade basics at the end of these lists.

Vegetables

ARTICHOKES: bay leaves, coriander, garlic, oregano, paprika, parsley, thyme

ASPARAGUS: basil, chives, dill, garlic powder, marjoram, mustard, nutmeg, oregano, rosemary, tarragon

BEETS: allspice, basil, caraway, chives, cloves, coriander, cumin, dill weed, ginger, mint, sage, star anise, thyme, tarragon

BELL PEPPERS: basil, cayenne pepper, coriander, garlic, oregano, paprika, rosemary

BROCCOLI: basil, chives, dill, garlic, ginger, marjoram, nutmeg, oregano, paprika, chili flakes, rosemary, sage, savory, thyme, turmeric

BRUSSELS SPROUTS: caraway, garlic, marjoram, mustard, nutmeg, oregano, parsley, rosemary, thyme

CABBAGE: allspice, bay leaf, caraway seeds, chives, garlic, ginger, marjoram, mint, nutmeg, parsley, thyme, turmeric

CARROTS: allspice, basil, bay leaves, caraway seeds, cardamom, cinnamon, coriander, cloves, cumin, dill, garlic, ginger, mace, mint, nutmeg, paprika, parsley, rosemary, sage, star anise, tarragon, thyme

CAULIFLOWER: basil, chili flakes, chives, coriander, cumin, dill, garlic, ginger, mint, nutmeg, oregano, paprika, parsley, sage, tarragon, thyme, turmeric

CELERY: allspice, basil, coriander, marjoram, nutmeg, paprika, thyme

CORN: basil, cardamom, cayenne pepper, chives, cilantro, cumin, dill seed, garlic, oregano, paprika, rosemary, thyme

CUCUMBER: basil, chives, coriander, dill weed, parsley, mustard, mint, rosemary, tarragon

EGGPLANT: basil, cayenne pepper, cilantro, cumin, garlic, ginger, marjoram, oregano, parsley, sage

GREEN BEANS: basil, chili flakes, chives, dill, nutmeg, garlic, black pepper, mustard, oregano, rosemary, thyme

MUSHROOMS: bay leaves, chili flakes, coriander, cumin, garlic, ginger, oregano, parsley, marjoram, mustard, nutmeg, rosemary, sage, tarragon, thyme

ONIONS: caraway seeds, chili flakes, coriander, garlic, mustard, nutmeg, oregano, parsley, rosemary, sage, thyme

PEAS: basil, cardamom, dill, mint, nutmeg, parsley, rosemary, sage, tarragon, thyme, turmeric

POTATOES: basil, bay leaves, black pepper, caraway seeds, cayenne pepper, chili flakes, chives, coriander, dill seed, dill weed, garlic, mustard, oregano, paprika, parsley, rosemary, sage, thyme, turmeric

RADISHES: basil, chives, dill, garlic, mint, parsley

SQUASH: allspice, cardamom, chili flakes, cinnamon, cloves, cumin, garlic, ginger, nutmeg, paprika, rosemary, thyme, sage

SWEET POTATOES: allspice, cardamom, chili flakes, cinnamon, cloves, garlic, ginger, nutmeg, paprika, thyme, turmeric

TOMATOES: basil, bay leaves, black pepper, cayenne pepper, chives, chili flakes, cilantro, cloves, coriander, cumin, dill, garlic, mint, oregano, paprika, rosemary, tarragon, thyme

ZUCCHINI: basil, black pepper, cayenne pepper, chili flakes, chives, cumin, dill weed, garlic powder, marjoram, oregano, savory, thyme

MEATS

BEEF: allspice, basil, black pepper, bay leaf, caraway, cayenne pepper, chili flakes, coriander, cumin, fenugreek, garlic, ginger, marjoram, mustard, oregano, rosemary, sage, thyme

LAMB: allspice, basil, bay leaf, cinnamon, cloves, coriander, cumin, garlic, juniper berries, marjoram, mint, nutmeg, oregano, paprika, parsley, rosemary, sage, savory, tarragon, thyme

CHICKEN: anise, basil, bay leaf, cardamom, cayenne pepper, celery seed, chili flakes, chives, cinnamon, cilantro, coriander, cumin, dill weed, fenugreek, garlic powder, ginger, lovage, mace, marjoram, mustard, oregano, paprika, parsley, rosemary, saffron, sage, savory, tarragon, thyme, turmeric

FISH: anise, basil, black pepper, bay leaf, caraway, cayenne pepper, celery seed, chervil, chives, cinnamon, coriander, cumin, dill, garlic powder, ginger, lemongrass, marjoram, mint, mustard, oregano, paprika, parsley, rosemary, saffron, sage, tarragon, thyme, turmeric

PORK: allspice, anise, basil, cardamom, caraway, celery seed, cinnamon, cloves, coriander, cumin, dill, garlic, ginger, juniper berries, mustard, paprika, oregano, rosemary, sage, savory, tarragon, thyme

TURKEY: basil, black pepper, chili powder, chives, coriander, cumin, garlic, marjoram, oregano, rosemary, saffron, sage, star anise, tarragon, thyme

VENISON: bay leaves, black pepper, cayenne pepper, chili flakes, cumin, garlic, juniper berries, marjoram, mustard, rosemary, sage, savory

MARINADE BASICS

After these meat seasoning suggestions, it seems fitting to go over some keys to creating a memorable marinade. A marinade is a balanced and flavor-packed mixture that consists of fats, acids, and seasonings.

Seasonings can include more than just spices and herbs. Sugars, soy sauce, and highly aromatic veggies like onions, shallots, and garlic can also serve as seasonings. Salt is important to have in the mixture, namely sea salt since it provides more diverse minerals and flavor hints. Soy sauce is popularly used instead of salt in a marinade. Keep in mind that salt pulls moisture so you do not want the marinade to be overly salty (you wouldn't want this for taste reasons either). Just as important though, remember that salt should be added to meat when it is still raw for better distribution, so it is necessary at this step. Any aromatic vegetables used for seasoning should be cut finely to increase surface area and overall contact with what you are marinating.

Fats used can range from olive oil and animal fats to coconut milk and even yogurt. These fat sources moisturize, enhance, and add their own subtle taste to the marinade mix.

Good examples of acids include citrus juices, wine, vinegars, and some fruits rich in enzymes. Acids in the marinade help to break down the surface of the meat but not much beyond this. Marinades do not do a great job of really tenderizing cuts of meat as many believe. A brine will be more effective at tenderizing. Acids also play an antioxidant role. If you want to decrease acidity while still making an impact, try zesting a citrus fruit into the marinade. The zest will provide a high flavor payoff without the extra acid content.

Honey, brown sugar, and agave nectar can all be used to add a nice dimension to marinades by boosting caramelization and balancing out the acidity. Sugars hold up best to low and slow cooking.

The actual ratio or balance between these essential marinade components is often left to taste since there are several schools of thought and preferences. In general, make sure oil content is higher than acid content. Meats with too much exposure to acid for too long can turn to mush on the outer layers. Seasonings should generously cover the food you are marinating since some will inevitably remain in the container after you remove it for cooking.

Don't be too rigid with measurements. Think in terms of general proportions. Getting lost in precise measurements will dampen your creativity and willingness to try something different. With time and familiarity, you will get a "feel" for how much to add. This is true for cooking with spices and herbs in general, not just for marinade creation.

PROCESS

While meats are marinating, they should be covered and in a container that is not reactive. Avoid aluminum; this will impart bitterness and can even lead to a metallic taste. Glass containers and re-sealable plastic bags work best. Bags can be especially useful because you can turn the bag over to help distribute the contents, and you will have more efficient storage. Meats should marinate in the refrigerator, but they can typically be taken out and left to sit at room temperature for up to an hour prior to cooking.

Meats like beef and pork can be marinated for hours or even a day or more in some cases. As stated previously, acid content should be taken into account. For whole birds and very thick roasts and cuts of meat, consider using a brine or dry rub instead of a marinade. Thinner cuts like steaks, chops, and portions used in stir fries are more ideal for marinating. Fish is much more delicate; it only needs to marinate for about 15 to 30 minutes at most.

If marinating softer vegetables such as squash and zucchini, 15 minutes is also a reasonable time frame. For other vegetables, 30 minutes will do the trick.

For safety, never keep a used marinade for later use. If you want to retain some for basting or for a pan sauce, reserve some of the marinade mixture for this purpose when you first create it.

Trying new ingredients in a marinade is another way to discover flavors unique to specific cuisines. For example, Indian marinades often incorporate acids like lime juice, spices such as coriander, and yogurt as a fat source. Thai marinades can include ingredients like lemongrass, chiles, and coconut milk. In marinades with a North African flare, you'll probably find components such as acidic lemon juice, and seasonings such as cinnamon or fenugreek. Honey is a popular sweet addition to North African marinades.

CHAPTER 6
SPICE SUBSTITUTIONS

If a recipe calls for a spice or herb that you do not have or use frequently, you can successfully substitute it. Though the recipe will not have the exact flavor originally intended, these replacements will not vastly change the overall dish and will blend into the flavor profile.

By learning some of these substitutions, you will save your original meal plan and become a more adaptable home cook in the process. You can even help a friend in a culinary pinch and ideally be able to vouch for the quality of the end-product.

If you are feeling a bit hesitant, a safe approach for using a substitution is to start with just half of the specified amount. Then, be sure to taste and adjust to suit your preference. Many of the suggested substitutions listed can be used as a 1:1 ratio with the spice you are replacing, unless noted otherwise.

ALLSPICE: cinnamon, nutmeg, mace, cloves

Tip: For 1 tsp allspice use ½ tsp cinnamon + ¼ tsp ground cloves + ¼ tsp nutmeg

ANISE SEED: fennel seed, anise stars, a few drops of anise extract

Tip: For ½ tsp anise seed use 3-4 Anise Stars

BASIL: oregano or thyme

CARDAMOM: ginger or ground cinnamon

CHERVIL: tarragon or parsley

CINNAMON: nutmeg, allspice

Tip: For 1 tsp use ¼ tsp nutmeg or allspice

CORIANDER: ground caraway seed, cumin

CHILI POWDER: dash of hot pepper sauce and a combination of oregano, cayenne, cumin, garlic

Tip: For 1 Tbsp use 2 tsp cumin + 1 tsp cayenne + 1 tsp oregano + ½ tsp garlic powder

CHIVES: scallions (chopped and reduced by half) or leeks (chopped)

CILANTRO: parsley

CINNAMON: nutmeg or allspice (use on ¼ of recipe amount if using allspice)

CLOVES: allspice, cinnamon, nutmeg

CUMN: chili powder

GARLIC: substitute 1 fresh clove for 1/8 tsp garlic powder, ½ tsp jarred minced garlic, ½ tsp garlic salt, ½ tsp garlic juice or 1 tsp garlic paste

GINGER: allspice, cinnamon, mace, nutmeg

Tip: Ginger, fresh grated (1 Tbsp grated): 1 tsp ground ginger + ¼ tsp white pepper + ½ tsp lemon juice

JUNIPER BERRIES: Juniper berries (6-10 crushed): 2 bay leaves + 1 tsp caraway seeds + 1 chopped mint leaf

MACE: allspice, cinnamon, ginger, nutmeg

MARJORAM: basil, thyme, savory

MINT: basil, marjoram, rosemary

MUSTARD: wasabi powder, horseradish powder

Tip: Use ¼ to ½ of recipe mustard quantity in wasabi powder

NUTMEG: cinnamon, ginger, mace

OREGANO: thyme, basil, marjoram

PARSLEY: chervil

Tip: For 1 Tbsp fresh, chopped: use ½ tsp dried parsley flakes

RED PEPPER FLAKES (CHILI FLAKES): dash hot pepper sauce, black pepper, cayenne pepper

Tip: For 1 tsp red pepper flakes substitute ½ tsp ground cayenne pepper

ROSEMARY: thyme, tarragon, savory

SAFFRON: turmeric

SAGE: savory, marjoram, rosemary

SAVORY: thyme, marjoram, sage

SESAME SEEDS: finely chopped blanched almonds

TARRAGON: chervil, fennel seed, anise seed

THYME: basil, marjoram, oregano, savory

TURMERIC: dash saffron (coloring), dry mustard powder

VANILLA: vanilla, almond, or soy milk, maple syrup, almond extract (half of recipe amount)

Chapter 7
Popular Spice Blend Recipes

Having delicious and well-balanced spice blends available in your kitchen is always an advantage. These blends will quickly create the signature taste and aromas of the international dishes you are craving.

You can also create a house spice blend for your own kitchen and use it as restaurants do—your versatile mix can enhance anything from roasted potatoes and meats to salads and vegetable medleys. Review Chapter 5 to get started on ideas for your own blend. Experiment to find something original!

Below you will find easy recipes for popular spice blends from around the world. Just mix and place in an airtight container. By mixing up these favorites on your own, it will be easier to make slight adjustments to suit your preferred taste.

Don't forget to apply some of the preparation, measurement, and storage tips you have learned. For convenience, most of these recipes include dried herbs and spices and their respective measurements. However, you can use fresh herbs instead, particularly if you plan to use the blend soon and the cooking time will be minimal within the intended dish or recipe. As for spices, keep in mind that you can toast them for even more flavor, before or after grinding or crushing.

Refer to Chapter 4 to review the tips for toasting spices, dried to fresh conversions, and more. You can also take another look at the marinade section in Chapter 5 to create some mouth-watering marinades using the diverse blends below.

Adobo

Caribbean

Recipe:

4 Tbsp paprika

3 Tbsp black pepper

2 Tbsp onion powder

2 Tbsp oregano

2 Tbsp cumin

1 Tbsp chili powder

1 Tbsp garlic powder

1 Tbsp turmeric

1 Tbsp salt

BAHARAT

Middle Eastern

Recipe:

4 Tbsp black pepper

3 Tbsp paprika

2 Tbsp coriander

2 Tbsp cinnamon

2 Tbsp ground cloves

1 Tbsp ground star anise

3 Tbsp cumin

1 tsp cardamom

4 tsp nutmeg

BLACKENED SEASONING

Cajun

Recipe:

2 Tbsp paprika

1 Tbsp cayenne pepper

1 Tbsp onion powder

2 tsp garlic powder

1 tsp black pepper

1.5 tsp sea salt

1 tsp dried basil

1 tsp dried oregano

1 tsp dried thyme

Bouquet Garni

French (Recipe below for dried herbs but is great fresh)

Recipe:

4 Tbsp dried parsley

2 Tbsp dried thyme

1 Tbsp dried and ground bay leaf (or 2 whole dried leaves)

2 Tbsp dried rosemary

2 Tbsp dried marjoram

*wrap in double layered square of cheesecloth and tie with kitchen twine before placing in dish for slow cooking (use enough twine for removal from pot prior to serving dish).

Chili Powder

Latin American

Recipe:

2 Tbsp paprika

2 tsp oregano

2 tsp garlic powder

1.5 tsp cumin

1.5 tsp cayenne pepper

¾ tsp onion powder

Curry Powder

Indian

Recipe:

2 Tbsp ground coriander

1.5 Tbsp cumin

1 Tbsp ground turmeric

2 tsp ground ginger

1 tsp dry mustard

1 tsp black pepper

1 tsp cinnamon

1 tsp cardamom

½ tsp cayenne or ground chiles

FINES HERBES

Mediterranean

Recipe *(best fresh):*

2 Tbsp parsley

2 Tbsp chervil

2 Tbsp chives

1 Tbsp thyme

1 Tbsp tarragon

GARAM MASALA

Indian

Recipe:

1 Tbsp. cumin

2 tsp ground coriander

1.5 tsp ground cardamom

1.5 tsp black pepper

1 tsp cinnamon

½ tsp ground cloves

½ tsp nutmeg

½ tsp cayenne pepper

HERBS DE PROVENCE

French

Recipe:

3 Tbsp thyme

2 Tbsp rosemary

2 Tbsp savory

2 Tbsp basil

2 Tbsp parsley

2 Tbsp oregano

2 Tbsp dried lavender flowers (optional)

1 Tbsp fennel seeds

1 Tbsp marjoram

1 Tbsp tarragon

ITALIAN SEASONING

Italian-American

Recipe:

2 Tbsp basil

2 Tbsp oregano

2 Tbsp rosemary

2 Tbsp marjoram

1 Tbsp thyme

1 Tbsp savory

1 Tbsp chili flakes

1 tsp garlic powder

JERK SEASONING

Caribbean

Recipe:

1 Tbsp. onion powder

1 Tbsp garlic powder

1 Tbsp brown sugar

1 Tbsp parsley

2 tsp cayenne pepper

2 tsp paprika

2 tsp salt

2 tsp black pepper

2 tsp thyme

1 tsp ground allspice

½ tsp chili flakes

½ tsp cumin

½ tsp nutmeg

½ tsp cinnamon

PICKLING SPICE

North American

Recipe:

1 Tbsp whole mustard seeds

1 Tbsp whole allspice berries

1 Tbsp whole coriander seeds

1 Tbsp red pepper flakes

1 Tbsp black peppercorns

1 tsp ground ginger

1 tsp nutmeg

2 bay leaves, crumbled

2 cinnamon sticks, crumbled

6 whole cloves

QUATRE EPICES

French, Mediterranean

Recipe:

2 Tbsp white pepper

1 Tbsp ginger

1 Tbsp nutmeg

1 tsp allspice or ½ tsp cloves

RAS EL HANOUT

North African

Recipe:

2 tsp nutmeg

2 tsp coriander

2 tsp cumin

2 tsp ginger

2 tsp salt

2 tsp cardamom powder

1 tsp turmeric

1 tsp cinnamon

1 tsp sugar

1 tsp paprika

1 tsp pepper

1 tsp cayenne pepper

1 tsp allspice

¼ tsp cloves

ZA'ATAR

Middle Eastern

Recipe:

1 Tbsp thyme

1 Tbsp cumin

1 Tbsp coriander

1 Tbsp toasted sesame seeds

2 tsp marjoram

2 tsp sumac

1 tsp black pepper

½ tsp salt

Printed in Great Britain
by Amazon